Three Kings Day
A Celebration at Christmastime

by Diane Hoyt-Goldsmith

photographs by Lawrence Migdale

Holiday House • New York

Library of Congress Cataloging-in-Publication Data
Hoyt-Goldsmith, Diane.
  Three Kings Day: a celebration at Christmastime / by Diane
Hoyt-Goldsmith ; photographs by Lawrence Migdale.— 1st ed.
    p. cm.
    Includes index.
  ISBN 0-8234-1839-1 (hardcover)
  1. Epiphany—United States—Juvenile literature. 2. Puerto Ricans—United States—Social
life and customs—Juvenile literature. 3. United States—Social life and customs—Juvenile
literature. [1. Epiphany. 2. Holidays. 3. Puerto Ricans—United States.] I. Migdale,
Lawrence, ill. II. Title.

BV50.E7H69 2004
263'.915—dc22   2003067625

Acknowledgments
We would like to thank Felipe and Jackie Rangel and their children, Veronica, Rebecca, and Andy, for their participation in this project and for their never ending hospitality. We are also grateful to Elsie Alvarado for her help, cooperation, and insights into the holiday in Latin America.
  We are grateful to Josefina Monter and Wanda Quiñones for their help in the early stages of our research and for introducing us to the Rangel family.
  Thanks to Luis Román for sharing his experience as a *santero* with us.
  We are especially grateful to Ursula Pizzini for the invitation to attend the Feast of the Epiphany services at the Westside Presbyterian Church in Manhattan, and to the Reverend José Lantigua and the Reverend Alistair Drummond for their help and cooperation.
  Thanks also to the *parranda* musicians: Enrique Torres (*güiro*), Angela Rodriquez (*cantante*), Maria Narvaez (*cantante*), William Vasquez (*guitara*), Herman Figueroa (maracas), Emelio Narvaez (*cantante*), Tino Narvaez (*guitara*), Alejandro Negron (*cuatro*), and Quique Ayala (*cuatro*), who made it all happen.
  We are indebted as well to the men honored to represent the Three Kings in the parade sponsored by El Museo del Barrio: Jesus "Papoleto" Melendez, a recipient of the 2001 Fellowship in Poetry from the New York Foundation for the Arts and a poet of El Barrio; Felix Lopez from Washington, D.C., the regional director of the Puerto Rican Federal Affairs Department; and José Ramon Olmo-Olmo, a journalist and facilitator for CUNY's Boriqua College.
  We thank Rolando Cortez and Chimayna Valdez for allowing us to photograph them with their *santos*.
  We would like to thank those who helped us learn about Puerto Rican customs along the way: Robert Cabrera and Natalia Cana-Cabrera for sharing their fabulous *vejigante* mask; Elena Martinez and all the people at Citi Lore, including Rosa Elena Egipciaco, a national treasure and *mudillo* expert, and the ladies in her class: Wanda Quiñones, Eva DeJesus, Yasmin Hernandez, Delia Perez, Ruth Burgos, and Yolanda Hernandez.
  Thanks also to the students in Veronica's class, to her teacher, Mrs. Consuegra, and to the principal of the Eastwood Elementary School, Dr. Aura Gangemi.
  Thanks also to Barbara Lopez and her family for their help in the early stages of our research and to Andrea Hernandez for her help and advice.
  A very special thank-you to all the people at El Museo del Barrio, who made working on this project such a delight: to the director, Julián Zugazagoitia, for allowing us to photograph in and around the museum; and especially Monica Tavares in education, who made learning about this holiday so much fun.

El Museo del Barrio has sponsored the Three Kings Parade for more than twenty-five years. The mission of El Museo del Barrio is to present and preserve the art and culture of Puerto Ricans and all Latin Americans in the United States. Through its extensive collections, varied exhibitions and publications, bilingual public programs, educational activities, and festivals and special events, El Museo educates its diverse public in the richness of Caribbean and Latin American arts and cultural history. By introducing young people to this cultural hertitage, El Museo is creating the next generation of museum goers, while satisfying the growing interest in Caribbean and Latin American art of a broad national and international audience. For more information please contact El Museo del Barrio, 1230 Fifth Avenue, New York, New York 10029, (212) 831-7272, www.elmuseo.org.

Christmas is over but ten-year-old Veronica and her family are getting ready for another holiday, *Día de los Tres Reyes,* or Three Kings Day. Also called the Feast of the Epiphany, it celebrates a Bible story from the New Testament. With the birth of Jesus, a bright star appears in the sky. Three wise men from distant lands follow the star, each bringing a special gift for the baby Jesus.

Veronica comes from a rich cultural background. Her father's parents are from Puerto Rico, and her other grandmother was born in Ecuador.

Veronica's father tells the story of the Three Kings. His version comes from a Puerto Rican storyteller and has become a family favorite.

Like Veronica's family, Latino people from all over South America and the Caribbean celebrate Three Kings Day. For many Latinos, Christmas lasts for twelve days, beginning with *Noche Buena* (Christmas Eve) on December 24. It continues with *Navidad* (Christmas), *Año Nuevo* (New Year's Eve and Day), and finally *Día de los Tres Reyes* (Three Kings Day) on January 6.

The Legend of the Three Kings

Long ago, at the time of the first Christmas, people all over the world worried about their problems and had important questions that needed answers. Three wise men from different countries noticed an unusually bright star in the sky. Being wise men, or Magi, they thought the star meant something special. They hoped it would lead them to the answers they were seeking.

One of the wise men was Balthazar. In his country, people had lost faith, or *fe*. Balthazar wanted to bring faith back to his people. When he saw the star, he thought that following it would help him to do so. He asked the other wise people in his kingdom to help him choose a gift—a symbol of the faith that had been his people's greatest quality. They had no faith now. Finally, the poorest beggar said, "Bring gold." So Balthazar did.

The second wise man was Melchior. In his kingdom, people were suffering because they had lost hope, or *esperanza*. Doubt, the great destroyer, had entered their hearts. Melchior also thought the star might lead him to an answer. He, too, wanted to bring a gift, but none of his advisers had any ideas. Then an orphan girl suggested he bring a carved bottle full of myrrh, the sweetest and spiciest of perfumes. So Melchior did.

The third wise man, Gaspar, was a king from Africa. His country was great because his people were blessed with *caridad*, or generosity. For years, however, selfishness had corrupted his people. Gaspar hoped to bring back generosity by following the star. A poor, hungry man suggested incense for a gift. Gaspar chose frankincense, the sweet incense of generosity.

Each king started off alone, but their paths joined, so they continued on together. In Bethlehem, the star shone the brightest and the sweet odors of pine and cedar filled the air. Soon a tall carpenter stood before them. They asked him where to find the answers they were seeking. The carpenter, whose name was Joseph, told them that he didn't know, but that they could lodge with his family.

Then Joseph brought them to the stable where the baby Jesus lay sleeping in a manger. The kings realized that Jesus was a great new king, and the answer to their problems. They knelt, giving their gifts with joyful hearts.

Returning home, each king felt a sense of peace and contentment. They were amazed, however, that their knapsacks were very heavy, even though they had given away their gifts. Each opened his sack to find not only the gift he had brought, but the gift of each other king as well—*fe*, *esperanza*, and *caridad*.

Three Kings Day is important because, for the first time, unbelievers had recognized a new kind of king. Finding answers to their spiritual questions, the Three Kings came back with the qualities of good Christians everywhere— faith, hope, and generosity.

Traditions of the Celebration

Three Kings Day was brought to the Western Hemisphere by the Spanish. In 1493, on his second voyage to the New World, Cristopher Columbus claimed the island of Puerto Rico for Spain. Only a few Spaniards settled there until 1815, when many people from Catalonia and the Canary Islands came to work in the highlands on the coffee farms. These new settlers brought many traditions. Christianity and Three Kings Day were new to Puerto Rico, but already a treasured part of European culture. Three Kings Day is celebrated in Spain and other parts of Europe today.

Veronica and her family live next door to her grandmother in a two-family house in Queens, New York. For the holidays, they like to decorate the house with lots of Christmas lights.

Veronica's grandmother helps the children decorate boxes to leave under their beds for the Three Kings.

Veronica, her sister Rebecca, and their brother Andy learned about Three Kings Day from their parents and their grandmother from Ecuador. When Veronica's grandmother was a little girl, the children who did not receive gifts from Santa Claus on Christmas waited until January 6, when the Three Kings paid a visit.

They put their shoes under their beds, as well as some grass in a little box. Then, in the middle of the night, the Three Kings came. Their camels ate the grass, and the kings left a small gift for each child.

Veronica and her sister and brother want to leave some grass under their beds like their grandmother did when she was a child. Unfortunately, New York is cold and snowy in January. They cannot find any fresh grass to put in their boxes. Their grandmother says they can leave a little water in a cup for the kings' camels instead.

In Puerto Rico, where Veronica's father, Felipe, grew up, Three Kings Day is a major holiday. Nearly everyone there celebrates it—with parties, gifts for the children, and even a *desfile*, or parade, through the streets to the village church. Now that he is grown and has children of his own, Felipe tries to re-create some of the best parts of the holiday for them.

Felipe laughs when he tells his children that in Puerto Rico, the kings never came on camels. They always rode on horseback, because no one has ever seen a camel in Puerto Rico.

When Veronica's father was a little boy, he put his shoes out for the kings on January 6. Although he enjoyed the little gifts he received, what Felipe remembers most is the fun and sense of community that the celebration brings.

Veronica and Rebecca go shopping for the holidays with their mother near their home in Queens.

Puerto Rico means "rich port" in Spanish, and it was originally the name of the main city and largest port on the island. Today that city is called San Juan and it is the capital of Puerto Rico.

Puerto Rico is an island in the Caribbean about one thousand miles south and east of Florida. It was a part of Spain for about four hundred years. It became a part of the United States in 1898 at the end of the Spanish-American War.

Puerto Rico is not a state, however. In 1952, Puerto Rico became a commonwealth of the United States. As such, it is self-governing. Its residents are U.S. citizens, although they do not vote in national elections or pay any federal income taxes. The first language of Puerto Rico is Spanish.

The 3.5 million Puerto Ricans come from many different ethnic backgrounds. In addition to the settlers from Spain, thousands of enslaved Africans were brought to the island in the early 1800s to work on the sugar plantations along the coast. Even before the Spanish came, there were native people on the island. For about two thousand years, Puerto Rico was populated by the Taíno people, also called the Arawak Indians.

The Taíno people were farmers, fishermen, and hunters. They made beautiful clay pottery. Many of their pots were decorated with simple drawings of mountains, animals, and spirits. The Taíno also carved images into large rocks and on cave walls. Some people believe that these symbols were a type of alphabet.

By the end of the sixteenth century, however, nearly all the Taíno had been killed in wars of conquest or had died of new diseases brought by Europeans to the islands. Some survivors married the Spanish newcomers, so there are people of Taíno ancestry in Puerto Rico today. There are many sites in Puerto Rico where the artifacts of the earliest native people can be seen.

Veronica and Rebecca look at artifacts from Taíno: Ancient Voyagers of the Caribbean *during a visit to El Museo del Barrio in New York City.*

The settlers of Puerto Rico were mostly Roman Catholics who held strong beliefs in saints. In those days, people made wooden replicas of the saints called *santos*. These were small enough for an altar at home or for a niche in the wall of a village church. Because the settlers lived in the remote mountains, it was hard for them to convince a priest to live there. So people came to rely on the *santos* during their prayers and rituals. They prayed to the *santos* for help and comfort.

Folk artists called *santeros* carved figures of saints from wood. Carvers learned their craft by observing other carvers. They often used homemade knives and tools.

During the celebration of Three Kings Day, many Puerto Ricans put their *santos* of the Three Kings in a special place of honor in their homes. On the eve of January 6, many carry their *santos* in a procession to the village church for a blessing.

Veronica's family has a collection of santos *depicting the Three Kings made by* santeros *in Puerto Rico. For the holiday, they are all on display in their home.*

During the holidays, Veronica visits Luis Román, a family friend. He is a santero who makes carvings of the Three Kings. His workshop is in the basement of the apartment building where he lives.

13

(Facing page) In the week before Three Kings Day, many children such as Veronica attend workshops at El Museo del Barrio. Veronica paints a mask of one of the kings.

(Left) Veronica decorates the king's paper crown with shiny plastic jewels.

(Top) Veronica tries on the finished mask.

15

Veronica and her family enjoy a parranda *in the basement of the Westside Presbyterian Church in Manhattan.*

Music to Celebrate the Three Kings

Three Kings Day wouldn't be the same without its music. In Puerto Rico, the Christmas holidays are not complete without a *parranda*—a spontaneous concert. On the evening of January 6, people with musical instruments gather outside the home of a friend. They play and sing until someone comes to the door to greet them. Tradition demands that the homeowner thank the musicians with something to eat or drink. Then, the musicians move on to the next house.

More often than not, people come out to join the celebration. As the evening progresses, the group gets bigger and bigger. Soon this band of musicians and singers fills the streets. A *parranda* is also called an *asalto*, because the musicians "assault" their listeners, demanding their attention and participation.

Puerto Rico has many kinds of music. *Jíbara* music is from the highlands, where most of the Spanish lived. It relies on stringed instruments such as guitars. *Plena* and *bomba* are musical traditions from the coastal regions and are influenced by African rhythms and drumming. Instruments such as maracas and the *güiro* show the influence of the Taíno.

(Left) The cuatro *is a type of small guitar developed in Puerto Rico.*

(Right) Maracas are made from dried gourds that have seeds inside.

(Left) The güiro, *a rhythm instrument, is made from a hollowed-out gourd. A musician plays it by stroking it with a metal comb.*

(Right) The cantantes, *or singers, are an important part of the* parranda.

The musicians play *aguinaldos,* or Christmas carols. Many of these tell the story of the Three Kings. Accompanied by different folk instruments, *aguinaldos* are a favorite part of every child's celebration. Instruments such as the *güiro,* guitar, maracas, and *cuatro* are common. Some of the folk songs of Puerto Rico are improvised—they are poems or songs with a simple rhythm that are made up on the spot.

When Puerto Ricans brought the celebration of Three Kings Day to New York, the *parranda* took on a different character. Most Puerto Ricans in New York live in high-rise apartment buildings. It isn't easy to stand outside and sing to your friends. In addition, the weather is cold in January and it often snows. But the *parranda* tradition persists because people find ways to make it work. Now a *parranda* often takes place indoors. Sometimes it is held in the basement of a church or in the hallway of a large apartment building.

(Top) Veronica's aunt Ursula welcomes people of all ages to the special Three Kings party.

(Right) Like the rest of the children who attend the party in the church basement, Veronica receives a gift from the Three Kings.

Veronica and her family enjoy a special meal on the evening before Three Kings Day.

After church, on the evening before Three Kings Day, Veronica and her family eat a special meal. On the menu are dishes that they have just once a year—such as the roast pork called *lechón hornado*. It is made with lots of garlic and spices such as oregano and achiote. Then there is *arroz con gandules*, which is rice with pigeon peas, and everyone's favorite—*pasteles*, a kind of Puerto Rican-style tamale. For dessert, there is *arroz con dulce*, a sweet rice pudding cooked in coconut milk.

*Before the Christmas season begins,
Veronica's parents prepare hundreds of* pasteles.
*Meats and spices are wrapped inside a dough
made with ground yautia root and green
bananas, and then steamed inside banana leaves.
Veronica's mother wraps the* pasteles *in
parchment paper and ties them with string.*
Pasteles *are offered to guests throughout the
Christmas holidays and especially on Three
Kings Day.*

A Recipe for *Arroz con Dulce*

Have an adult prepare the coconut by taking two
whole coconuts and chopping the tops off with a
sharp, heavy knife. Drain out the liquid and reserve.
Break the coconuts into small chunks with a hammer.
Using a table knife, an adult should insert the blade
between the shell and the coconut meat. Then twist
the blade to separate the coconut from the shell.

Grate the coconut or shred it in a food processor
with a little coconut milk and some water. Squeeze
and strain the mixture through cheesecloth. Reserve
the liquid and throw out the solids. This should
provide about 2 cups of coconut milk. (You can also
use canned coconut milk, available in specialty food
shops.)

Cook 3 cups of short-grained rice in 6 cups of
water until tender.

In a large pot, combine the coconut milk with these
ingredients:

1/2 teaspoon freshly grated ginger
1 teaspoon cinnamon
1/2 teaspoon ground cloves
1 teaspoon vanilla
A pinch of salt
1 cup sugar
1 cup brown sugar

Stir together and heat. Add 1 cup of raisins.

Bring the mixture to a boil. Then slowly add the
cooked rice to the pot. Stir continuously until the
mixture absorbs some of the liquid. The texture should
be a little soggy. Pour into a serving dish to cool.
Serve at room temperature and enjoy!

21

After dinner, Veronica visits a friend of the family named Wanda Quiñones. Wanda is an artist who makes little dolls called *muñecas folkloricas*. Each miniature doll is dressed in a traditional and finely detailed Puerto Rican costume. Most even have tiny masks to wear, made in perfect scale. The inspiration for her dolls comes from all the wonderful parades that celebrate holidays in Puerto Rico. Veronica tells Wanda all about the special parade she will be attending on Three Kings Day.

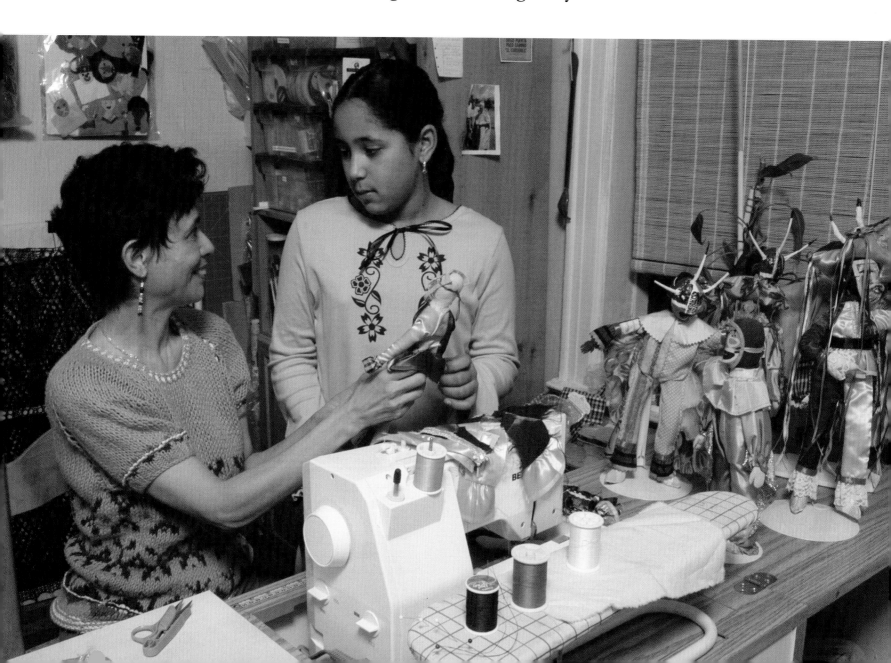

Three Kings Day Is Here!

On the morning of January 6, Veronica wakes up early. When she looks under her bed, she finds a small gift in the box that she left there. Her brother and sister are lucky to find a few presents too. Best of all, however, is that Veronica and her grandmother plan to go to the Three Kings Day Parade in Manhattan.

During the night, snow has fallen and it is bitterly cold. The radio is forecasting a heavy snowfall for the afternoon. So Veronica and her grandmother put on their warm winter coats and hurry out to reach the parade route before the crowds arrive.

Since 1977, El Museo del Barrio has sponsored the Three Kings Day Parade. The museum was created to highlight the art and culture of Latino people, whether their ancestors are from the Caribbean or from Latin America. Throughout the year, the museum has exhibits, special events, and educational programs for both children and adults. The Three Kings Day Parade is one of its most exciting events.

The parade was originally planned to celebrate the traditions of the Puerto Ricans living in Spanish Harlem, where the museum is located. Today the Three Kings Day Parade has grown to be one of the largest held in the United States.

Beginning outside the museum, several thousand schoolchildren follow a parade route that takes marchers on a loop through the neighborhood.

Veronica's brother, Andy, opens his box to find a small gift from the Three Kings.

(Top) A decorated banner announces the parade.

(Below) Camels and sheep follow Veronica and her grandmother as they walk in the parade.

El Museo del Barrio's 26th Annual

Three Kings Day Parade

January 6, 2003

24

(Top) Honored members of the Puerto Rican community play the Three Kings: (far left) Jesus "Papoleto" Melendez; (third from the left) Felix Lopez; and (fourth from the left) José Ramon Olmo–Olmo. Marching next to him is Michael Bloomberg, the mayor of New York City, and on the far right, musician Willie Colon.

(Below) Neighborhood schoolchildren wearing handmade paper crowns brave the cold to watch the parade.

(Top) Students from the neighborhood schools
have a good time marching in the parade.

(Left) People who live along the parade route
bring their santos out to greet the marchers.

Dressed in *the traditional costume of a* vejigante, *this marcher brightens a gray afternoon. In Puerto Rico, the* vejigante *is an important symbol during the celebration of* Carnaval.

(Top) The snow may be falling, but everyone is enjoying the day. Large papier-mâché figures of the kings are a festive part of the parade.

(Left) Veronica and her grandmother cheer as the kings pass through El Barrio.

(Top) After the parade, marchers are invited into the museum to meet the Three Kings. Musicians play aguinaldos. *The Nativity scene is made up of wooden carvings by many different folk artists.*

(Left) Before they leave for home, each child receives a gift from one of the Three Kings and the madrina, *or godmother (center), played by the director emeritus of El Museo del Barrio, Susana Torruella Leval.*

29

Veronica shares her composition on the Three Kings with her class.

On January 7, the twelve days of Christmas are over and it is time for Veronica to go back to school. As requested by her teacher, she brings along a composition about the celebration of Three Kings Day. Sharing what she has written with her class, she feels proud of her family and their heritage. It has been fun to experience the traditions of Puerto Rico and other parts of the Hispanic world. The celebration has put her in touch with the history of her ancestors—with her Hispanic roots. Already she is looking forward to next year.

Glossary

(All words in italic are Spanish.)

aguinaldo: (a gwee NAHL doh) A Christmas carol

Año Nuevo: (ahn yoh noo AY voh) New Year's Day on January 1

arroz con dulce: (ah ROHS con DOOL say) A dessert served during the Three Kings Day celebration made from rice cooked in sweet coconut milk

arroz con gandules: (ah ROHS con gahn DOO lays) A traditional Puerto Rican dish served on Three Kings Day made with rice and pigeon peas

asalto: (ah SAL toh) Used as a synonym for *parranda* because the musicians "assault" their neighbors with sound

Balthazar: (BAL thah zar) One of the Three Kings

barrio: (BAH ree oh) A neighborhood

Bethlehem: The place where Jesus was born

bomba: (bom BAH) Puerto Rican music from the coastal regions, influenced by African drumming traditions

cantantes: (can TAHN tays) Singers

caridad: (car-ee-DAHD) Generosity

Carnaval: (car nah VAL) A festival celebrated by people in the Caribbean, Latin America, and South America to commemorate the last days before Lent

cuatro: (KWAH troh) A four-string guitar

desfile: (des FEE lay) A parade

Día de los Tres Reyes: (DEE ah day los tres RAY yes) The celebration of the Feast of the Epiphany held on January 6 in the continental United States, in Puerto Rico, and in other countries in the Caribbean and Latin America

esperanza: (ES pay RAHN sah) Hope

fe: (fay) Faith

frankincense: A gum resin burned as incense, a valuable perfume in the ancient world

Gaspar: (gas PAHR) One of the Three Kings

güiro: (GWEE roh) An instrument made from a hollowed-out and dried gourd, and played by stroking with a metal comb

lechón hornado: (lay CHON hor NAH doh) Roast pork

Los Tres Reyes: (los tres RAY yes) The Spanish term for the Three Kings

madrina: (mah DREE nah) In Latino tradition, a godmother or woman who serves as a mentor or teacher

Magi: Another term for the wise men who came bearing gifts for Jesus

maracas: (mah RAH cahs) A percussion instrument made from small dried gourds with pebbles or seeds inside

Melchior: (mel CHOR) One of the Three Kings

muñecas folkloricas: (moo NYEY kahs fok LOR ee cahs) Small dolls dressed in folk costumes

museo: (moo SAY oh) A museum

musica jíbara: (MOO see kah ee BAR ah) The music of the Puerto Rican highlands, played with stringed intstruments such as guitars and *cuatros*

myrrh: (mur) A fragrant gum resin from Africa and Arabia used in incense and perfume

Navidad: (nah vee DAHD) Christmas Day on December 25

Noche Buena: (NOH chay BWEY nah) Christmas Eve on December 24

parranda: (pah RAHN dah) A spontaneous concert of street musicians on *Día de los Tres Reyes* that moves from house to house

pasteles: (pahs TEH lays) Puerto Rican-style tamales served during the Christmas season

plena: (PLAY nah) Music from the coastal regions of Puerto Rico, influenced by traditional African drum music

santero: (sahn TER roh) An artisan who creates *santos*

santo: (SAHN toh) The figure of a saint carved from wood

Taíno: (tah EE noh) Indigenous peoples of the Arawakan language group who lived in the Greater Antilles at the time when the Spanish explorers arrived in the Americas

vejigante: (bay hee GAHN tay) A person wearing a brightly colored costume and mask during *Carnaval* in Ponce, Puerto Rico

Index

(Numbers in italics refer to pages with photos or illustrations)